Good Places

poems by

Kathleen Henderson Staudt

Finishing Line Press
Georgetown, Kentucky

Good Places

Copyright © 2017 by Kathleen Henderson Staudt
ISBN 978-1-63534-095-2 First Edition
All rights reserved under International and Pan-American Copyright Conventions.
No part of this book may be reproduced in any manner whatsoever without written permission from the publisher, except in the case of brief quotations embodied in critical articles and reviews.

ACKNOWLEDGMENTS

"The Volunteer" appeared in *Ruminate* magazine, Winter 2012-13.
"Reveling" appeared in *Presence* magazine, March 2016.

Publisher: Leah Maines

Editor: Christen Kincaid

Cover Art: Kathleen Henderson Staudt

Author Photo: Lesley Anne Furlong

Cover Design: Elizabeth Maines

Printed in the USA on acid-free paper.
Order online: www.finishinglinepress.com
　　　　　also available on amazon.com

Author inquiries and mail orders:
Finishing Line Press
P. O. Box 1626
Georgetown, Kentucky 40324
U. S. A.

Table of Contents

The Volunteer 1
Evening on the Patio 2
Candle-Light 3
Patio Music 4
Seventeen-Year Cicadas: 2004 5
Viriditas: Three Meditations 6
Presences 8
Hummingbird 9
Broken and Beautiful 10
Ordinary Times 11
Unknowing 12
Emptying the Wrenhouse 14
House Blessing 15
All Souls Day 16
Autumn Tankas 17
Thanksgiving 18
Stanzas for Advent 19
Dancing Day 20
Epiphany Light 21
Seed-Time: An Oracle 22
Lenten Villanelle 23
Holy Saturday 24
Openings 25
Sestina for Spring 26
Hydrangea Season 28
A Corker of a Day 29
Changing 30
Crossing 31
Reveling 32
End Notes 33

*It is essential to experience all the times and moods
of one good place*

—*Thomas Merton*

The Volunteer

The tree sprang up, a volunteer
After we lost the shade
Of the oak tree that came down.
It grew out of a thicket
in a corner of the yard
during the busy years when we
were not paying attention.
Then suddenly one spring, at cherry blossom time,
The yard filled up with blooms.

Never invited, fed or tended
Now the upstart cherry tree
Spreads above the house
Offering its summer shade
Beyond the patio wall.

In June its fruits draw birds
Who stay to nest and grow.
All summer long its glossy leaves
Shelter hidden songs.

In August and September, as the cricket-song begins,
The cherry leaves are deepening to early autumn green
Then turning yellow, one by one, they drift to the earth
Early heralds of the season's turn

In winter, snow and icy drops along its naked limbs
Expose the gangly shape of a tangled, weedy tree
It branches without symmetry, unlovely, growing free.
We never would have chosen it or planted it there
Yet in February light, its bark shines silver-bronze
Reminding us of unsought gifts
That bring us what we need
Unplanted, untended, steadily there:
The grace that volunteers.

Evening on the Patio

Classes are over. It is June, and I breathe faint citronella scent, taste the sweet crunch of cold vanilla ice cream, sharp chocolate crust of a melting Klondike bar, my summer luxury. Solitary here, I rest and watch grey-green twilight, silhouettes of holly, rhododendron, and the darkening spruce, its pale cones shimmering as twilight comes. Catbirds call and squirrels chatter, high among the leaves. Bats flutter. Swallows dart across the silvering sky. A cardinal on a mulberry branch calls out to his mate, as fireflies twinkle on.

The night's first coolness brushes my skin, breaking the day's heat. I breathe in slowly, breathe in the summer, slowing down. Breathe and listen. Listen and rest.
Breathe.   Listen.   Rest.

Candle-Light

After the lights went out
In a summer thunderstorm,
Our small kitchen, by candlelight,
Became a place of safety.
And we, relieved to find ourselves together,
Stayed together.

On the radio, reports of accidents and fallen trees
Stretches of the beltway down to one slippery lane
"I'm glad you are home!" I say.

Washing cups by candlelight, we listen to the radio
Reports of earthquakes and tornado warnings, far away
And we, with food still warm, enough batteries and candles,
Children safely tucked in bed
With nothing to distract us,
        We talk.

I tell you of a moment
From my life outside this kitchen
A moment when I thought of you, wished you were there
And saved a thought to share.
        And you listen.

We talk of other families where anger eats away,
Or breaks out, uncontrolled, and deep hurt spreads.
But for now, we are not talking about ourselves.
        We are safe.

On the beltway, says the radio, a truck has skidded out
Near the exit on your way to work.
I kiss you on the forehead, in the candlelight,
        "I'm glad you are home," I say.

Patio Music

Out on the patio, surrounded by green
        after last evening's violent storm
                The air washed clean

I listen to wren song, crow caw, squirrel quarrel
        Wings flutter, tails scurry, chirp, peep, scold

Beltway traffic drones and roars
        White noise, half heard beyond the birds
              A low continuo.

Soothed by the cooing mourning doves
        I watch and listen here

On the patio, surrounded by green
        After last evening's violent storm
              The air washed clean

Seventeen Year Cicadas: 2004

We can't avoid them when they come
    A plague, some say
    of ugly bugs and deafening noise.
They dive-bomb on our picnics, die
    On patios and walks
    in piles of crunching wings.
Their fleeting lives remind us of the fleetingness of ours.

But as for me, I love their treetop wedding song
    They harmonize and whistle: *Wowwowwowwowwow*
I love to see their blunderbussy bodies whirligig
    on lacy wings, like fledgling angels practicing for heaven
They celebrate their lives in sussurating song,
    Breeding and dying, they promise a return
Mysterious, predictable, in seventeen years.

Who knows where I will be, or on what side of life
    the next time they are here.

I'm glad I have not missed them this time.

Viriditas: Three Meditations

I

The morning shines on the cherry leaves.
Green and glossy, they shine back
Taking in the light
That is their life .

In the hidden greenness of each cell
Sunlight changes into food
And now the leaves shine back

As one beloved, in the lover's gaze
Gives back the radiance of love received.

II

Flat light. Clouded late summer sky. Greying olive-greens. At first sight, the lively green that glowed on brighter summer days seems dulled today, monochrome.
But looking closer at the hues of green in every separate leaf, I can see soft contrasts in the deeper greens, nuances of color in amid the darker shade.   These are graying-greens, edging toward flat silver, subtleties that come with the season's maturity. Yes. The wise and graying greens of early August, the prime of summer's life, are most truly seen when morning light is dimmer, flatter, undistracting, as it is today.

III

In caritate, let me be
Like a fish in the ocean
Breathing the waves breaking over me

Let me be
Like a bird in the morning
Glistening on air, the sun warm on my wings

Let me be
A woman just passing the change of her life
Resting outside on her patio
Sipping Darjeeling, surrounded by green-ness
Listening to birdsong, soft breeze on her skin.

Presences

Sometimes, like a gift from the hidden world
A rare bird appears in my back yard
Simply, without fanfare,
As if it knew the place, belonged eternally
In the world that I can see
Just over the patio wall.

Like the goldfinch who arrived today,
Splendid among sparrows,
Perched there on the feeder
Just long enough for me to see
His stunning yellow-gold.

Or the family of owlets I heard screeching one evening
Just beyond the fence
And glimpsed in a holy moment:

A fledgling lumbered, shrieked and flapped
While its mother watched
Strong, serene, from her high perch
As if she were a guardian spirit
Always present, rarely seen.
Then both took off and disappeared
Back into the green.

From my patio I witnessed
Their huge rushings of white wings.

Hummingbird

A tiny hummingbird has made the rounds
this morning, from the cherry tree, across
the patio, and now she rests, so still,
on a branch of the blue spruce. Her energy
surrounds her when she hovers, like a veil
encircling, as she sucks and sips, suspended.
Visiting each scarlet flower, fuschia, zinnia,
she darts from bloom to bloom with a chipping sound,
delighted and delighting, without pause,
until each flower is visited, and then
as still as she was active, stops, and rests
right where I can see her.
And I am here
To see this hummingbird today.

Broken and Beautiful

This morning, by the birdseed can
Quiet on the gravel
A butterfly, a tiger swallowtail
Rested motionless
The pattern of his wings stretched out
Pale yellow, black stripes
And at the tail, that bright mosaic
Of shining royal blue.

I wondered why he stayed so still
Then I saw
He was broken: from one wing
A corner had been torn, or bitten off
This brokenness was why
He hadn't flown away
But lay there still for me to gaze upon.

Can you fly with that? I asked him, aloud.
I did not pick him up:
No intruding on his world.
But later, reading on the patio
I saw him flutter awkwardly
To a hidden branch
Broken and beautiful,
Safe and alive for now.

Ordinary Times

Long gone the afternoons watching from the patio, while children played on rickety swings, dug in the sandbox, invented games with dandelion puffs. Long gone.

First there were the daily routines. Crying times, naptimes, errands in between. We walked with the stroller to the park in the early evenings, stayed to play until the fireflies came out. Then there were the daily morning walks to the school bus, always with the same neighbors, days ordered by children's departures and returnings. Then came the carpool years, evening baseball games, music lessons, daily drives to new schools far away from home. Every day predictably, reliably hectic.

We marked the turning points with tears and celebrations. The last day of school. The first day of a new year. Commencements. Departures. We promised to remember, took pictures, wore our special clothes. But what happened on the last days before each turning, before the celebrations began? The patio days, like a Wednesday in the week-long beach vacation, when we have settled in and can take this day as it will come, because we know there will be more like it, and we don't have to count yet how long until the end. What happened to the last of those ordinary days?

Perhaps it is a blessing that we do not mark
the last day of ordinary time.

Unknowing

A few weeks from now we will move from here
To the new place we have chosen.
I will leave this patio, grey stone, red brick and green

Today I do not know what I will know soon
How much this house will sell for, when moving day will be
Who will live here next
I wonder how my morning solitary times will be
As we learn to live in our new place

Years ago, climbing Mount Olympia
We found ourselves surrounded
In thick fog. All that we could see
Was the path under our feet
And so we took the next step, and the next, hoping
That through the clouds, we'd come
To a sunlit view: white mountains, blue valleys
Wildflowers blooming purple pink.
But we could not know what we would see
Coming to that high place.

I lost my companions for a while, as the fog dropped.
They kept on striding, intent on the summit
But I slowed down
My steps took me only as far ahead as I could see.
Slowing, my mist-filled eyes began to see
What I might have missed, going faster:
By the side of the path, intense blue of mountain aster
Fire of devil's paintbrush
And tiny grey-green lichens, hanging on.

And so I pause now, at my fifty-ninth year
With mist-filled eyes
To gaze at where I am: grey stone, brick wall
The pink geranium where the hummingbirds have come
Chrysanthemums, burnt orange, on the patio wall
And the surrounding green that has been my home.
Not knowing what the move will make of me
When I come to our new place.

Emptying the Wrenhouse

The nest we watched them build
Twig by careful twig
Crumbles into compost now
Its work complete, except
To feed the future soil.

House Blessing

O Wisdom, without words,
meet me at your door.
Lead me to your dwelling place
book lined, and candle-lit
To the room where I can close the door
and be at home.

Show me out into the open hall
Where welcome guests will come
To feast and be at home
Around a table laid for all

Draw me out to the light filled space
Between rooftop and sky
Where treetops are companions
And birds come to be fed

Glassed in, skylit,
A thinned out place
Where I can meet each morning
Washed in light.

All Souls Day

Days of the dead this autumn
Follow the waning storm

I gaze up through the skylight
At the tulip poplar tree
Almost bare, its lingering leaves
Faded, yellow-brown.

Beside me, tops of feathered cypress trees
Grown tall, create a screen
Between us and our neighbors.
Evergreens will hedge me round
Every winter morning.

Quieted, protected, I look down to the yard,
Greet the day and the seasons ahead:
Seasons of elections, of thanks-givings
Home-comings, home-goings
Family and saints
Visiting, abiding here.

The mystery draws inward now
Sheltered from the chilling air
That streams between the dappled clouds
Of this November sky.

Autumn tankas

pale grey sky shines cold
through the tulip poplar tree
branched above the house
thick buds closed among dead leaves
shelter next spring's shade

the tree stands rooted
older than all these houses
it guards and blesses
holds a space for lasting life
as the world thins out

a flock of starlings
high above the darkening trees
pulses as one body
shape shifting, soaring southward
through the autumn sky

blue jays on grey boughs
hop and peck for seeds
perch on faded yellow vines
tangled among evergreens
blue and beautiful.

Thanksgiving

The redeye from the coast came in on time.
No traffic from the airport
The beloved grown-up child is now asleep upstairs.

The turkey warms on the countertop.
I have peeled a garlic clove,
Sliced up pungent onions,
Chopped celery and carrots, pulled out the turkey neck
And stock is boiling now.
I rub into the turkey skin
Butter, sage, and thyme. Then let it rest awhile
And I rest, too, with a morning cup of tea.

I make the white sauce for the cauliflower now
Remembering my grandmother, who said "be sure
Your butter has melted, before you add your flour, and
Add it slowly.   Pay attention.
Cook the milk until it just begins to smoke:
Don't let it boil. Then stir
the smooth, thick sauce."

She did not add:
Every time you do this
You will remember me.

Stanzas for Advent

Here in this thin place
a single advent candle
burns in a balsam wreath.
Winter storms promised
but today the air is still.

The dormant season
shelters invisible seeds.
Bare maples and tulip poplars
stand in their true shapes
beside the cypress trees.

Now a lady house finch
darts across the quiet air.
She is all motion
like the violin that bursts
from a web of harmony
in a late Beethoven string quartet.

I watch her stirring into flight
and now the cypress hedge begins
to swivel in the rising
wind of the coming storm.

A house that welcomed many
now makes a place for me.
Windows from floor to ceiling
let in pale dawn light
on white-trimmed earthtone walls.

The candle flame casts
shadows from the driftwood cross
across the icon. Eyes gaze out
Angel wings and halos glow
out of the heart of Love.

Dancing Day

> *Sing O my love, O my love, my love, my love*
> *This have I done for my true love. . . .**

I awoke one Christmas Eve
Startled into joy
And for a moment
Saw the story whole

The One who made us, who is
Love, impassioned for us
Will not be kept out
By our indifference

But bursts through all the barriers
Human and divine
Takes our trembling flesh

Is held, bloody and wailing,
Swaddled tight in wondering arms,
Knows
Longing, satisfaction
Hunger, thirst, distress
As we know these things: firsthand and loving us

Knows, embraces
All.

It is a dancing day indeed
The moment this begins.
Creation, coming whole again,
Gathers in
All the broken pieces
Lost, beloved, found.

Always there is a gathering, a dancing going on.
We move with gracefulness between
Dailiness and Mystery
Words made flesh
Singing back the song.

Epiphany Light

Our Christmas feast has passed.
Morning light reveals
A house returned to normal.
Ornaments and lights,
Cloth of red and green
Now put away until next year.

January morning light
Glows like the lining of a shell.
The year has turned. The light returns.
Though the trees are bare
And walkways patched with ice,
Spring seems possible.

Furniture of ordinary months
Re-ordered, in its place
invites the day's work now, and I
begin again, settled in quiet joy.

Seed-time: An Oracle

This is the seed-time: Be, like the seed, and wait.
When unseen rain seeps through the dark loam,
Crack open, release the first tiny shoots.
Let them reach up to drink, grow, drink again.

Feel the rich soil. Crack once more,
And stretch down roots to hold you there.
You will be changed, as the shoots push up toward the sun,
Greeting the birds of the air.

As the seed is lost in growing, reaching, rooting,
So you may not know yourself.
You cannot foresee the fruit or the flower.
   Only be, like the seed, and wait.

Lenten Villanelle

It seems too soon to let the winter go
The season turns, but still I want to stay
Something is stirring, deep beneath the snow.

The barren landscape beckons me to slow
My walking, notice hues of gray.
It seems too soon to let the winter go.

The grey of beech bark gives a silvery glow
As clinging dry leaves rustle, shine and play
Something is taking root beneath the snow

Days lengthen, and the light begins to grow
More springlike. In the holly, robins play
It seems too soon to let the winter go.

The early signs of life emerge now. Slow
Forsythia buds and snowdrops want to say:
Something is stirring, deep beneath the snow.

In winter's bareness, words have space to grow.
I'll welcome spring's abundance, But today
It seems too soon to let the winter go
Something is taking root, and stirring, deep beneath the snow.

Holy Saturday

Rain. Strong, steady April rain
Scatters waning blossoms on the grass
Invites scarlet tulips, yellow daffodils
To stiffen, open, rise

In churches that observe this day
Everything is grey
Crosses gone or covered, candles out
Waiting for the night when New Fire flames
Baptized, Exultant, Singing.

This is the waiting time.
Whatever happened during Lent
Is buried in the harrowed soil
It puts down roots now, drinking in
The steady April rain
Who knows what green will grow
From this quiet, rain-soaked day?

Openings
> *—"and the leaves of the tree are for the healing of the nations."*   *—Revelation 22:2*

In the fullness of time
When all is restored and made whole
Perhaps we shall see
What we only glimpse now, from time to time.
This place, this world
Open to the fullness
Of God's *kairos* time

An image I am given
The New Creation already complete
Within the world, as in the physicists'
Extra dimension, parallel to ours.
Perhaps we are brushing up against it all the time,
Witness
Moments of inbreaking, unveiling, *apocalypse*,
When, for an instant, all is held
In wholeness, loving and alive.

As I write this
I am sitting on the high porch of a new home,
Listening to the rain
Whose cleansing showers will soon complete
The budding of the unfamiliar trees.

All around me, here above my deck,
Above my neighbors' rooftops,
I see the not-yet moments of early spring:
Cherry blossoms on the verge of opening
And the redbuds out. Now begin
The growing hints and sprinklings of green.

Soon I will know for sure
The names of these trees,
Written on the leaves that are budding now
Out of the brown nobs on bare limbs.
Soon I will know their names.

Sestina for Spring

This is the first day weeding my new garden
Hands in the earth, I dig at stubborn roots
Of dandelion, grasses and deep green
Burdock and pokeweed, listening to the songs
Of the red cardinal, on the budding branches.
His insistent love song tells that spring is here

I watch to see what will be growing here
What is already living in this garden
New to me. I watch for leaves on branches
Of trees and shrubs that have their roots
Deep in the yard, and now I hear the songs
Of courting wrens among the evergreens.

Now through a wash of lacy yellow green
I recognize by name the new leaves here
The signatures of maple, ash, green songs
Written in the leaf-shapes of the garden.
I dig my hands in deeper now, touch roots
Of weedy vines that clog the space with branches.

The tap root from the wild grape vine whose branches
Spread out and tangle into vines of green
Choking treetrunks, and sending smaller roots
Throughout the soil, yields to my shovel here.
Triumphant, I pull out the vines, freeing the garden
For new planting, as birds call out their songs

Spring peepers now begin their evening songs
As daylight fades, hidden among the branches
Of tulip poplar trees above the garden.
The cypress hedge, a darkening shade of green
 Surrounds the yard, protective, saying "here
 Is your new place, where you will grow new roots."

And indeed I have begun to put down roots
In this new space, where every morning songs
Of cardinal, wren and chickadee tell us, here
We are now, in this place, where branches
Budding, soon mature to summer's green
To shade us as we tend and plant this garden.

And so I pause, rejoicing to be here
Beneath the shading branches, birdsong, green
Putting in new seeds, new roots, in my new garden.

Hydrangea Season

Blue hydrangeas:
A miracle of color—bold against the green
And settled, somehow, always coming back
As if they were ordinary flowers in summer dooryards
But who could imagine this deep purple-blue
Blue like the clearest mid-June sky
On a washed clean morning
Against deep green. Not yet
Faded by the wilting heat
They shimmer with news of summer.

A Corker of A Day

"A corker of a day," you used to say
On days like this—late summer, early fall
Or fresh, bright mornings in Maine or Colorado:
A day to be outdoors,
Breathe in clear air,
Admire a shining sky and lively trees
That startle with their beauty:
Early-reddening maples,
Tall, cool pines on granite mountain rocks
Or quiet oak trees, deepening green, alive with hidden song.

I doubt I ever said these words aloud, myself.
They were your own; now they live on in me.
Today, when for a moment I forgot
How you've been gone now for so many years,
I spoke them out, and longed to turn to you, and say
Look, Dad. Isn't this
A corker of a day!

Changing

The tulip trees that spread
Above the neighborhood
Are just beginning, now, their autumn change

Still green, but coppery,
with just a hint of gold
The gold that soon will cover everything

Like salt and pepper grey
In an old friend's dark hair
Heralding the quiet wisdom of age

Rooted in long living
Soon to be transformed
All over, into silver that will shine.

Crossing

Nearing the threshold of my seventh decade
I set out for a walk, this crisp September morning

It is the first day of school today,
And even though my children are long grown and gone
I feel again the season's promise, as I walk
Past mothers and children at school bus stops.

At the driveway to the international school,
Traffic is busy. I pause to watch
As well-dressed parents from around the world
Emerge from SUV's with their children, hand in hand.

The crossing guard, Nigerian, turns toward me.
He sees me lingering, raises his hand,
And says, with deep respect,
Mama, will you cross now?

Mama: that's the name
Of the wise women at the church,
Older and wiser, I have always thought, than I
Mama, they are called by the younger men,
Preserving the courtesies of African life.

"Mama," says the guard, as he holds up his hand
I am holding the cars for you: will you cross?
"Mama, will you cross?" He is speaking to me.
Renamed, I am crossing now.

Reveling

Prayer, Teresa said, will finally be
A simple conversation between friends.
Beyond the drama and the wilderness
The dry places and the upwelling springs
At last, or intermittently, we settle
To daily conversation. That is all

And sometimes, as today, the conversation
Lapses. Nothing, really, now, to say
And even though the silence might appear
To be an invitation into some
Dramatic mystic moment, it is not
Exactly that. Rather, a simple reveling:
Contentment without content: resting in
The quiet being-here that long love brings

Endnotes

In caritate; Literally—"In love" but the grammar of Latin, with the noun (caritas) in the "ablative case", deepens that "in" so that "in love" means something more like "sunk into" or "surrounded by" love.

Carol: "Tomorrow will be My Dancing Day," in William Sandys, *Christmas Carols Ancient and Modern* (London: Richard Beckley, 1833), 110.

Trained as an academic, **Kathleen Henderson Staudt** (Kathy) has read and studied poetry for most of her life, writing a scholarly book and many articles on the work of the Anglo Welsh Catholic poet and artist David Jones . She began writing poetry herself at mid-life and has found that the practice of poetry has become a spiritual practice of attention, enabling her to dwell deeply in the richness and the challenges of life, loss, relationships and transitions. In her first volume of poems, *Annunciations: Poems out of Scripture* (2003), she explores the way that stories from the Bible, especially (though not exclusively) the New Testament, have come alive for her and illuminated important life experiences. In *Waving Back: Poems of Mothering Life*, also published by Finishing Line Press, the poetry takes her through the years of child-rearing, exploring along the way themes of healing, celebration, loss and letting go. The current volume, *Good Places*, traces a physical journey between places, a journey that quietly becomes a time of spiritual transformation. Leaving an old home and moving to a new, these poems explore the experience of being fully present in a place, finding in the trees, the garden, the birds, light and interior spaces of an old home and a new home images for losses and the discoveries, the turnings and the seasons of life.

www.ingramcontent.com/pod-product-compliance
Lightning Source LLC
LaVergne TN
LVHW041555070426
835507LV00011B/1088